THIS BOOK BELONGS TO...

Name:	Age:

Favourite player:

2022/2023

My Predictions...	Actual...

The Seagulls' final position:

The Seagulls' top scorer:

Premier League winners:

Premier League top scorer:

FA Cup winners:

EFL Cup winners:

Contributors: Peter Rogers, Andy Greeves

A TWOCAN PUBLICATION

©2022. Published by twocan under licence from Brighton & Hove Albion FC.

Every effort has been made to ensure the accuracy of information within this publication but the publishers cannot be held responsible for any errors or omissions. Views expressed are those of the authors and do not necessarily represent those of the publishers or the football club. All rights reserved.

ISBN: 978-1-914588-65-5

PICTURE CREDITS: Action Images, Alamy, Brighton & Hove Albion FC, Paul Hazlewood, Press Association

£11

CONTENTS

GOAL
OF THE
SEASON

The Albion midfielder had two goals in contention for the award, the other being our second goal in the 2-1 win at Arsenal, but few could argue that his stunning effort in the 2-2 draw at Liverpool deserved top billing. Picking up the ball on the right, he hit a curling, first-time effort that flew over Alisson and into the back of the net to give the Seagulls a lifeline before half-time.

"My teammates were asking whether I meant it, even the Liverpool players were asking me at the end of the game, but of course I meant it – I had planned the goal before the game!" he recalled with that beaming smile of his. "On the bus going to Anfield, I was watching clips of Yaya Toure and the way he scored when he got into those areas – goals with curve, precision and power.

"It's always a difficult shot for goalkeepers to stop, so I thought to myself that if I get into those positions, I would try to do the same. Again, I only had one thing in my mind and that was to shoot. It was a fantastic feeling to see it go in. For it to be my first Premier League goal made it even more special."

Mwepu scored three times in a debut campaign that was interrupted by injury. Still, he made 17 Premier League appearances and enjoyed his first season in Sussex.

"I'm enjoying the challenge, the competitive nature of the league – it's a dream come true to be playing here," added the former RB Salzburg midfielder. "I think my game is suited to the football in England and I hope to keep showing what I can do to the gaffer and the fans and to keep on improving."

ENOCK
MWEPU

NUMBER OF SEASONS
WITH THE SEAGULLS:

5

BRIGHTON & HOVE ALBION
LEAGUE APPEARANCES:

162

BRIGHTON & HOVE ALBION
LEAGUE GOALS:

90

PLAYER OF THE SEASON WINNER:
2000/01 & 2001/02

LEGEND

BOBBY ZAMORA

SEAGULLS ACHIEVEMENTS:

Football League Third Division winners
2000/01
Football League Second Division winners
2001/02

MAJOR STRENGTH:

Quick turns and change of pace to get
past defenders into goalscoring positions

INTERNATIONAL ACTION:

Zamora won two England senior caps - both
under Fabio Capello - during the squad
rebuild after the country's dreadful showing
at the 2010 FIFA World Cup in South Africa

FINEST HOUR:

Finishing top scorer in each
of the club's title-winning seasons

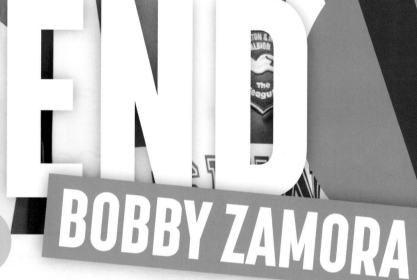

**Bobby Zamora and Glenn Murray are two players
who will be remembered for their ruthless nature
in front of goal.**

True target-man strikers, the pair were most prolific
in their Brighton days, despite both representing
a host of different teams throughout their careers.

But which of the two frontmen was better?

LEGEND

GLENN MURRAY

NUMBER OF SEASONS WITH THE SEAGULLS:

8

BRIGHTON & HOVE ALBION LEAGUE APPEARANCES:

287

BRIGHTON & HOVE ALBION LEAGUE GOALS:

111

PLAYER OF THE SEASON WINNER:

Never

SEAGULLS ACHIEVEMENTS:

Football League One winners 2010/11

EFL Championship runners-up 2016/17

MAJOR STRENGTH:

Perfecting the aggressive target-man playing style which frightened defences

INTERNATIONAL ACTION:

Murray had no international appearances despite a glittering career in the English leagues

FINEST HOUR:

Netting his 100th goal for the Seagulls against Wolves in October 2018

9

ADAM
LALLANA
14

Defending is not just about stopping the attackers and clearing your lines. Making the best of possession you have just won is vital - although the danger has to be cleared, it is important for your team to keep hold of the ball.

SOCCER SKILLS
LONG PASSES

When passing your way out of defence, and short, side-foot passes are not possible, the longer pass, driven over the heads of midfield players, can be used.

EXERCISE

In an area 40m x 10m, A1 and A2 try to pass accurately to each other, with a defender B, in the middle between them. Player B must attempt to stop the pass if possible, and A1 and A2, must keep the ball within the area of the grids.

After each successful long pass, the end player will exchange a shorter pass with B before passing long again, thus keeping the exercise realistic and also keeping the defender in the middle involved. The player in the middle should be changed every few minutes, and a 'count' of successful passes made for each player.

KEY FACTORS

1   Approach at an angle.
2   Non-kicking foot placed next to the ball.
3   Eye on the ball.
4   Strike underneath the ball & follow through.

Practice is the key to striking a consistently accurate long pass and to developing the timing and power required.

The same end result could be achieved by bending the pass around the defender instead of over him, and this pass could be practised in the same exercise, by striking the football on its outer edge (instead of underneath) which will impart the spin required to make the ball 'bend' around the defender - not an easy skill!

11

PREMIER LEAGUE
2022/2023
SQUAD

1 ROBERT SANCHEZ

GOALKEEPER   DOB: 18/11/97   BIRTHPLACE: SPAIN

A youth-team player with Levante in his homeland, Rob moved to the Albion in June 2015. To gain first-team experience, he joined Forest Green Rovers on loan in 2018/19, making his debut in a 4-1 win at Grimsby Town. He made 17 League Two appearances before stepping up a division to join Rochdale the following season. The highlight of his time at Spotland was a Carabao Cup tie at Manchester United, where he gained plenty of plaudits with the game going to penalties.

He returned to Sussex ahead of the 2020/21 season and following a pre-season injury sustained to Christian Walton, was promoted to the first-team squad. On 1st November he made his debut for the club, in a 2-1 defeat against Tottenham. He soon established himself as the Seagulls' first-choice 'keeper – with Mat Ryan joining Arsenal on loan as a result – and penned a new contract in February 2021. His excellent form was rewarded with a call-up to the Spain squad and he made his debut in September 2021 in a World Cup qualifier against Georgia.

2 TARIQ LAMPTEY

DEFENDER   DOB: 30/09/00   BIRTHPLACE: ENGLAND

Tariq came through the ranks at Chelsea, joining the club's academy at the age of eight. He went on to make his Premier League debut, as a substitute, against Arsenal at the Emirates Stadium in December 2019 - and played a key role as the Blues came from behind to win 2-1.

He joined the Albion the following month, but had to bide his time to break into the first team. It duly arrived at Leicester City that June, where his marauding runs helped the Seagulls to a solid 0-0 draw. Be it in the full-back or wing-back position, his pace has been a real asset for the Seagulls when either attacking or defending – and he now has over 50 club appearances to his name.

4 ADAM WEBSTER

DEFENDER   DOB: 04/01/95   BIRTHPLACE: ENGLAND

A player who featured in all three EFL divisions with first club Portsmouth, Adam made his debut against West Ham United in the Championship, aged 17, in January 2012. He went to appear 81 times for the club before a move to Ipswich Town in June 2016. He spent two seasons in the second tier with the Blues, then switched to Bristol City, where he was crowned the club's Player of the Year in his one season at the club.

The centre-back joined Albion from the Robins in August 2019 and soon became one of the first names on the team sheet. He made his Premier League debut that same month at Manchester City and also gained praise from Pep Guardiola for a subsequent performance at the Etihad Stadium. Adam, who has now made over 90 Premier League appearances, is a former England under-19 international with six caps to his name.

5 LEWIS DUNK

DEFENDER **DOB:** 21/11/91 **BIRTHPLACE:** ENGLAND

While the club captain is Brighton born and bred, he actually started his football career with Wimbledon, but left when the Dons relocated to Milton Keynes. He joined Albion's centre of excellence at under-12 level and progressed through the ranks to make his senior debut in a League One encounter at MK Dons in May 2010. He made a further five league appearances the following season, as the Seagulls won the title, before emerging as a first-team regular in the club's debut campaign at the Amex Stadium.

A commanding presence at centre-half, 'Dunky' has gone on to make over 380 appearances for the Seagulls and his form in the Premier League was rewarded with an England debut against the United States in November 2018. There have been calls for a return to the Three Lions' set-up and in 2020/21 Dunk's imperious displays for the Seagulls were rewarded with a second successive Players' Player of the Season award.

6 LEVI COLWILL

DEFENDER **DOB:** 26/02/2003 **BIRTHPLACE:** ENGLAND

Joining Chelsea at under-9 level, the centre-back, who can also operate on the left side of defence, spent the 2021/22 season on loan at play-off chasing Huddersfield Town in the Championship.

He made 29 league appearances, scoring twice, as the Terriers reached the final against Nottingham Forest. An England U21 international, he joined the Seagulls on a season-long loan in August and made his Premier League debut as a late sub in a 2-1 win against Manchester United on the opening day of the season.

PREMIER LEAGUE
2022/2023
SQUAD

7 SOLLY MARCH

MIDFIELDER   DOB: 20/07/94   BIRTHPLACE: ENGLAND

Solly had spells at Crystal Palace and Eastbourne Borough before making his competitive debut playing for Isthmian Premier League club Lewes, in September 2011, against Aveley. Soon after, he joined the Albion, despite interest from Millwall and Newcastle, and linked up with the development squad. He was voted the club's Young Player of the Season in 2013 and went on to make his debut that August in a 2-1 Championship defeat against Derby County.

March has made over 240 appearances for the Seagulls – and netted one of the goals which secured promotion to the Premier League, against Wigan, in April 2017 – but 2020/21 was, arguably, his best to date in a blue and white shirt. Employed by ex-boss Graham Potter as a left wing-back, he showed great form and consistency until sustaining a knee injury in the memorable win at Liverpool which curtailed his season. Named by Gareth Southgate in the England under-21 squad in May 2014, March went on to make three appearances, scoring once against Denmark.

8 ENOCK MWEPU

MIDFIELDER   DOB: 01/01/98   BIRTHPLACE: ZAMBIA

Albion's first signing of the 2021/22 campaign, Enock arrived from Red Bull Salzburg on a four-year contract. He began his career with Kafue Celtic in his homeland and moved to Austria in the summer of 2017, where he was immediately loaned out to feeder club Liefering in the Austrian First League.

He returned the following season to establish himself in the RB first team and also made a Champions League debut against Liverpool, at Anfield, in 2019/20. His Albion debut came on the opening day of last season at Burnley and he went on to make 21 appearances, scoring three goals, including the club's Goal of the Season in a 2-2 draw at Liverpool. A Zambia international, he has made 23 senior appearances for his country, scoring six goals.

10 ALEXIS MAC ALLISTER

MIDFIELDER **DOB:** 24/12/98 **BIRTHPLACE:** ARGENTINA

Alexis comes from a footballing family, with his father Carlos a former left-back for Boca Juniors and the Argentina national team, while his older brothers Francis and Kevin are also professionals. He started out in the Argentinos Juniors' youth set-up and went on to make his senior debut in October 2016 against Central Cordoba. He appeared 33 times in the Primera Division, scoring five times, before joining the Albion in January 2019. As part of the deal, he was immediately loaned back to Argentinos Juniors, before joining his brother Kevin at Boca Juniors that summer.

He appeared in ten league games for the Argentine giants, scoring twice, before a return to England. A Premier League debut came shortly before the COVID-19 pandemic hit the country, against Wolves in March 2020, but Alexis's breakthrough campaign came in 2020/21, where he appeared 21 times in the top flight and netted a memorable 90th minute equaliser at rivals Crystal Palace. He has since featured regularly for both club and country.

11 LEANDRO TROSSARD

MIDFIELDER   **DOB:** 04/12/94   **BIRTHPLACE:** BELGIUM

A member of the Genk academy, 'Leo' was promoted to the senior squad in 2012 and made his debut that year against Gent. His breakthrough season came in 2016/17 and he went on to make over 80 appearances in the Belgian top flight. His performances in the 2018/19 helped Genk to the title and he was crowned the league's Player of the Year, having scored 14 goals. The winger joined Albion that June and netted on his Premier League debut against West Ham at the Amex.

He has since made over 100 Premier League appearances, scoring 20 goals, including eight goals in the 2021/22 season. While he had been a member of the Belgium squad before his arrival in Sussex, Leandro made his debut for the Red Devils in a Nations League game against Denmark in September 2020. He was also a member of Belgium's Euro 2020 squad, making his first appearance in the 2-0 group stage defeat of Finland.

13 PASCAL GROSS

MIDFIELDER   **DOB:** 15/06/91   **BIRTHPLACE:** GERMANY

Following in the footsteps of his father, Stephan, who played professional football for Karlsruher, Pascal made his Bundesliga debut for Hoffenheim, in a 4-0 defeat to Wolfsburg in May 2009. Having made five top-flight appearances, he moved to his father's former club, where he emerged as a regular in Bundesliga 2 in the 2011/12 season. That summer he was on the move again, to fellow second-tier club FC Ingolstadt, playing a key role in their promotion in 2014/15.

He remained a regular for the following two seasons before joining the Seagulls ahead of the club's debut Premier League campaign. He made history by scoring Albion's first ever Premier League goal, in a 3-1 win against West Bromwich Albion that September. Pascal went on to make his 100th appearance in an EFL Cup tie at Preston in September 2020, where he was made captain. He signed a new two-year contract in the summer of 2022.

17

14 ADAM LALLANA

MIDFIELDER   **DOB:** 10/05/88   **BIRTHPLACE:** ENGLAND

A member of the AFC Bournemouth centre of excellence, Adam joined Southampton's academy as a 12-year-old in 2000. He went on to make his debut in a League Cup win against Yeovil Town in August 2006 before establishing himself in the first team in 2008/09. The central midfielder went on to become a key player as the club won successive promotions to the Premier League in 2012, and his form in two top-flight seasons clinched a move to Liverpool.

While at Anfield, he was a member of the squad that won the Champions League in 2019 and picked up a Premier League winners' medal the following season. Heading back south with the Seagulls in the summer of 2020, he came off the bench to help the side to a famous 1-0 win at Anfield in February 2021, and has since made over 50 top-flight appearances for the Albion. Having won 34 England caps, Lallana was named the Three Lions' Player of the Year in 2016.

15 JAKUB MODER

MIDFIELDER   **DOB:** 07/04/99   **BIRTHPLACE:** POLAND

In 2014, Jakub joined Lech Poznan's academy and by April 2018 he had made his first-team debut in a 3-1 win at Wisla Krakow. His breakthrough campaign in the Polish top flight came in 2019/20, where he made 26 appearances, scoring five goals, as the side finished runners-up and qualified for the Europa League. In October 2020, he joined the Albion but was immediately loaned back to his former club. He returned to Sussex following the club's exit from the Europa League and went on to make his Albion debut in an FA Cup tie at Leicester in February 2021.

An impressive 2021/22 season was cut short in April when Jakub sustained a cruciate knee ligament injury, all but ruling him out of the World Cup with Poland. Having made his international debut in a Nations League defeat against the Netherlands in September 2020, he scored a memorable second goal for his country at Wembley, against England, in March 2021.

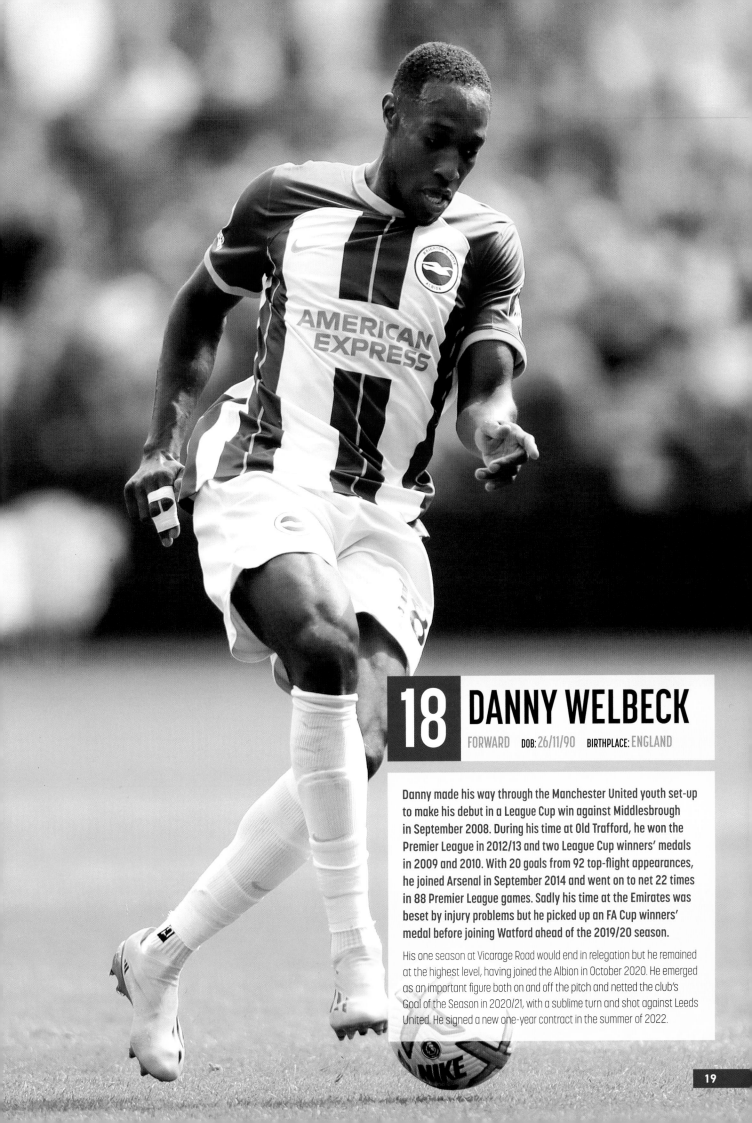

18 DANNY WELBECK

FORWARD   DOB: 26/11/90   BIRTHPLACE: ENGLAND

Danny made his way through the Manchester United youth set-up to make his debut in a League Cup win against Middlesbrough in September 2008. During his time at Old Trafford, he won the Premier League in 2012/13 and two League Cup winners' medals in 2009 and 2010. With 20 goals from 92 top-flight appearances, he joined Arsenal in September 2014 and went on to net 22 times in 88 Premier League games. Sadly his time at the Emirates was beset by injury problems but he picked up an FA Cup winners' medal before joining Watford ahead of the 2019/20 season.

His one season at Vicarage Road would end in relegation but he remained at the highest level, having joined the Albion in October 2020. He emerged as an important figure both on and off the pitch and netted the club's Goal of the Season in 2020/21, with a sublime turn and shot against Leeds United. He signed a new one-year contract in the summer of 2022.

19 JEREMY SARMIENTO

FORWARD   **DOB:** 16/06/2002   **BIRTHPLACE:** SPAIN

Born in Madrid to Ecuadorian parents, Jeremy's family moved to England for work-related reasons and in 2009 he joined the Charlton Athletic academy. He remained with the Addicks until 2018 when he had the chance to join Benfica. He played UEFA Youth League football with the Portuguese giants before moving to the Albion in July 2021.

He went on to make his senior debut against Swansea in the EFL Cup that September, while his first Premier League start came against West Ham in early December. A former England youth international, he made his international debut for Ecuador in October 2021 against Bolivia.

20 JULIO ENCISO

FORWARD   **DOB:** 23/01/2004   **BIRTHPLACE:** PARAGUAY

Julio joined Paraguay Primera Division club Libertad when he was 11 and went on to make his senior debut on 17 March 2019, in a 4-0 win against Deportivo Santani. At the age of just 15 he became the youngest first-team player in the club's history.

Julio went on to make 55 top-flight appearances, scoring 18 goals, before joining the Albion in the summer of 2022. He made his international debut for Paraguay, in a Copa America win against Bolivia, in June 2021.

21 DENIZ UNDAV

FORWARD   DOB: 19/07/96   BIRTHPLACE: GERMANY

Deniz made a big impression with former club Royale Union Saint-Gilloise, where he scored 26 league goals last season. His form earned a move to the Albion in January 2022 and he was then loaned back to the Belgian top-flight club for the remainder of the season.

He finished the campaign as the league's top scorer and was also named the division's Player of the Year. Prior to his spell in Belgium, Deniz played for Meppen in the German third division.

22 KAORU MITOMA

FORWARD   DOB: 20/05/97   BIRTHPLACE: JAPAN

A graduate of the University of Tsukuba team, he made his professional bow with Kawasaki Frontale in 2020, establishing himself in the J League side following the return to action after the COVID-19 outbreak. The winger had an impressive first season, reaching double digits in terms of goals, and he went on to score 21 league goals in 50 appearances.

A move to the Albion followed in August 2021 and he was immediately sent out on loan to Belgian top-flight club Royale Union Saint-Gilloise, where he impressed as the side led the championship for much of the campaign.

23 JASON STEELE

GOALKEEPER **DOB:** 18/08/90 **BIRTHPLACE:** ENGLAND

A product of Middlesbrough's academy, Jason made his professional bow on loan at League Two Northampton Town, in February 2010, against Cheltenham Town. His Boro debut came that October against Chesterfield in the League Cup and he went on to make over 130 Championship appearances for the club. In September 2014 he joined Blackburn on a season-long loan deal, which was made permanent just three months later.

After three full seasons at Ewood Park, he returned to the north east, joining newly-relegated Championship side Sunderland, but featured just 18 times as the Black Cats were again relegated. In June 2018 he headed south to Brighton, and having emerged as the club's number two to Rob Sanchez, he has made nine first-team appearances, including a Premier League debut against Aston Villa in November 2021.

25 MOISES CAICEDO

MIDFIELDER **DOB:** 02/11/01 **BIRTHPLACE:** ECUADOR

The teenager arrived in Sussex from Ecuadorian top-flight side Independiente del Valle in February 2021, having made his professional debut in an Ecuadorian Serie A win over LDU Quito in October 2019. Last season proved to be his breakthrough in the centre of midfield, spending the first half of the campaign on loan at Belgian side Beerschot before returning to the Albion, where his Premier League debut came in the 2-1 win at Arsenal in April.

Moises made his first appearance for Ecuador in a 1-0 World Cup qualifying defeat to Argentina in October 2020 and scored the opening goal, a few days later, in a 4-2 win against Uruguay – becoming the first player born in the 21st century to score in CONMEBOL World Cup qualifying. He also appeared for his country at the Copa America in the summer of 2021.

27 BILLY GILMOUR

MIDFIELDER　　DOB: 11/06/2001　　BIRTHPLACE: SCOTLAND

Billy Gilmour joined Albion on a four-year deal from Chelsea in September 2022. The 21-year-old came through the ranks with Rangers, before making the move to Chelsea in 2017.

He made his Premier League debut aged 18 as a substitute against Sheffield United in 2019, before making two appearances in the Champions League in 2020/21 as Thomas Tuchel's team won Europe's biggest competition. Billy was an unused substitute in the final. He spent the 2021/22 season on loan with Norwich City, where he made 24 Premier League appearances. Billy made his debut for Albion three days after signing for the club, coming on as a late substitute in the 5-2 win over Leicester City.

28 EVAN FERGUSON

FORWARD　　DOB: 19/10/2004　　BIRTHPLACE: ROI

Evan made his first appearance for Bohemians in a pre-season friendly against Chelsea in July 2019, aged just 14. His competitive debut came that September and he made four appearances in two seasons with the club.

In January 2021, the forward joined Albion's academy and he made quick progress to the first team, with a debut coming that August in an EFL Cup tie against Cardiff City. The Republic of Ireland international went on to make his Premier League debut against Burnley in February 2022.

29 JAN PAUL VAN HECKE

DEFENDER DOB: 08/06/00 BIRTHPLACE: NETHERLANDS

A former youth-team player with VV Goes in his homeland, Jan joined NAC Bredia ahead of the 2018/19 season and went on to make his senior debut in a 5-1 Eerste Division win over Helmond Sport in August 2019. He went on to make 11 league appearances, scoring three goals, before joining the Albion on a three-year contract in September 2020.

He was immediately loaned out to Eredivisie club Heerenveen, where he made 28 league appearances. Last season was also spent on loan, this time to Championship club Blackburn Rovers, where his impressive form was rewarded with the club's Player of the Year award - the club's first loanee to receive the accolade.

30 PERVIS ESTUPINAN

DEFENDER DOB: 21/01/98 BIRTHPLACE: ECUADOR

The Ecuador international left-back joined the Seagulls in August 2022 from La Liga side Villarreal. He began his career with LDU Quito in his homeland before joining Watford in 2016.

To gain experience, he spent time on loan in Spain at Granada, Almeria, Mallorca and Osasuna, before joining the 'Yellow Submarine' in 2020. He has played 26 times for his country, scoring three goals, and will be hoping to be in the squad for the World Cup finals in Qatar.

34 JOEL VELTMAN

DEFENDER   **DOB:** 15/01/92   **BIRTHPLACE:** NETHERLANDS

A product of the Ajax academy, Joel went on to make his debut against NEC in August 2012. The following eight years saw him win three Eredivisie titles, the KNVB Cup and a Europa League runners-up medal against Manchester United.

A versatile player, who can play also play in midfield, he moved to Sussex in July 2020 and made his debut that September against Portsmouth in the Carabao Cup. While his appearances were more fleeting in the first half of the season, he established himself in the right wing-back position in 2021 - following the long-term injury sustained by Tariq Lamptey - and maintained a regular place in the side throughout the 2021/22 season. His form for the Seagulls cemented his place in the Netherlands' Euro 2020 squad, having made his debut for his country in November 2013 against Colombia. He was also a member of the Netherlands' 2014 World Cup finals squad.

MULTIPLE CHOICE

Here are ten Multiple Choice questions to challenge your footy knowledge!

Good luck...

ANSWERS ON PAGE 62

1. What was the name of Tottenham Hotspur's former ground?

A) White Rose Park
B) White Foot Way
C) White Hart Lane

2. Which club did Steven Gerrard leave to become Aston Villa manager?

A) Liverpool,
B) Glasgow Rangers
C) LA Galaxy

3. Mohamed Salah and Son Heung-min were joint winners of the Premier League Golden Boot as the division's top scorers in 2021/22.

How many goals did they score?

A) 23   B) 24   C) 25

4. What is the nationality of Manchester United boss Erik ten Hag?

A) Swiss   B) Dutch
C) Swedish

5. Where do Everton play their home games?

A) Goodison Road
B) Goodison Way
C) Goodison Park

6. From which club did Arsenal sign goalkeeper Aaron Ramsdale?

A) Sheffield United
B) Stoke City
C) AFC Bournemouth

7. What is Raheem Sterling's middle name?

A) Shaun
B) Shaquille
C) Silver

8. Who won the 2021/22 League One Play-Off final?

A) Wigan Athletic
B) Sunderland
C) Rotherham United

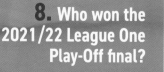

9. How many times have Brighton reached the FA Cup final?

A) Once
B) Twice
C) Three times

10. From which club did the Seagulls sign Danny Welbeck in 2020?

A) Manchester United
B) Arsenal
C) Watford

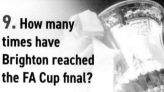

10

ALEXIS
MAC ALLISTER

ANSWERS ON PAGE 62

FAN'TASTIC!

Gully the Seagull is hiding in the crowd in five different places as Albion fans greet the players at the Amex. Can you find all five?

25

MOISES
CAICEDO

Close control in tight situations creates havoc in opposition defences - particularly when receiving the ball in the air - and nine times out of ten, when a striker receives the ball, he has his back to goal.

SOCCER SKILLS
RECEIVING THE BALL

Quite often the ball will arrive in the air, and good strikers have to be able to cope with that - controlling and turning in one movement, ready for the instant shot.

EXERCISE 1

In an area 20m x 10m, two players A and A2 test the man in the middle, B, by initially throwing the ball at him in the air, with the instruction to turn and play in to the end man - if possible using only two touches.

The middle player is changed regularly, and to make things more realistic, the end players progress to chipping the ball into the middle.

The middle player is asked to receive and turn using chest, thigh, or instep.

KEY FACTORS

1   Assess flight early - get in position.
2   Cushion the ball.
3   Be half turned as you receive.

EXERCISE 2

A progression of this exercise is the following, where the ball is chipped or driven in to the striker from varying positions. He has to receive with his back to goal, and using just two touches in total if possible, shoot past the keeper into the goal!

To make this even more difficult, a defender can be brought in eventually. For younger children, the 'servers' should throw the ball to ensure consistent quality.

31

TRAIN TO WIN

Making sure that you are fit, healthy and fully prepared is key to success in whatever challenge you are taking on. Those three factors are certainly vital for professional footballers and also for any young aspiring player who plays for his or her school or local football team. The importance of fitness, health and preparation are key factors behind the work that goes into preparing the Brighton players to perform at their maximum on matchday.

The Seagulls players will need to demonstrate peak levels of fitness if they want to feature in the team. Before anyone can think of pulling on a blue and white shirt and stepping out at the American Express Community Stadium, they will have had to perform well at the Training Ground to have shown the manager, his coaches and fitness staff that they are fully fit and ready for the physical challenges that await them on a matchday.

Regardless of whether training takes place at the training ground or at the stadium, the players' fitness remains an all-important factor. Of course time spent practicing training drills and playing small-sided games will help a player's fitness but there is lots of work undertaken just to ensure maximum levels of fitness are reached.

Away from the training pitches the players will spend a great deal of time in the gymnasium partaking in their own personal work-outs. Bikes, treadmills and weights will all form part of helping the players reach and maintain a top level of fitness.

Over the course of a week the players will take part in many warm-up and aerobic sessions and even complete yoga and pilates classes to help with core strength and general fitness. The strength and conditioning coaches at the club work tirelessly to do all they can to make sure that the players you see in action are at their physical peak come kick-off.

While the manager and his staff will select the team and agree the tactics, analysts will provide the players and staff with details on the opposition's strengths, weaknesses and their likely approach to the match.

Suffice to say the training ground is a busy place and no stone is left unturned in preparation for the big match!

YOUNG GUN

JEREMY SARMIENTO

Making his first-team breakthrough last season, 20-year-old Ecuador international Jeremy Sarmiento is the club's current Young Player of the Season and is set for a bright future with the Seagulls.

Jeremy, how does it feel to be voted the club's Young Player of the Season?

I really appreciate it. It's been a hard journey for me, coming from Portugal, but I've been given the confidence to play for the first team, which is something I've always dreamed of. The players have also made me feel at home and to have made my Premier League debut last season was a great feeling.

Given you only arrived in the summer of 2021, that's some rise, right?

I knew I'd be starting with the under-23s but I've ended up training with the first team, week in, week out, which I'm really, really proud of. Training among all these experienced players is really nice. They guide me through training and games and have been really supportive.

You made your senior debut in the Carabao Cup against Swansea. What was that like?

To be honest, I didn't expect it to come so quickly. What got me there was my performances for the under-23s, where I felt I did a good job for the team. To step out onto the pitch at the Amex for my debut was a great feeling and nice to have helped us win the game.

Then came your Premier League debut against Leeds. How good was that?

To come on against Leeds was amazing really. We had a sell-out crowd and I did feel kind of nervous, but as you get on the pitch that just goes. The crowd was buzzing and that really motivated me whenever I got on the ball. I only managed to get ten minutes but thought I did okay. I was buzzing afterwards.

What are your targets moving forward?

To keep impressing and keep getting more minutes under my belt. I'll back myself in any situation, so if I keep doing well, then hopefully I can play more games. The team is heading in the right direction and I want to be a part of that. I also want to keep my place in the Ecuador squad, which is an honour for me every time I am called up, but I know there's lots of hard work ahead.

DREAM TEAM

Pick your ultimate Brighton & Hove Albion
dream team and design them a kit!

PASCAL
GROSS
13

PREMIER LEAGUE
DANGER MEN

20 TOP-FLIGHT STARS TO WATCH OUT FOR DURING 2022/23...

ARSENAL
GABRIEL JESUS

The Gunners completed the signing of Brazilian international striker Gabriel Jesus from Premier League champions Manchester City in July 2022.

A real penalty-box predator, Jesus netted 95 goals in 236 appearances in a trophy-laden spell for City and Arsenal will be hopeful he can continue his impressive goals-to-games ratio at the Emirates Stadium.

ASTON VILLA
EMI BUENDIA

Now in his second season at Villa Park, following a big money move from Norwich City, a great deal will be expected of Argentinean international midfielder Emi Buendia in 2022/23.

A highly skilful and creative player, Buendia has the ability to create chances for teammates and score vital goals himself.

BOURNEMOUTH
KIEFFER MOORE

Giant front-man Kieffer Moore chipped in with four goals in three games to help Bournemouth secure promotion to the Premier League last season.

The former Cardiff City man will be keen to prove his worth at Premier League level in 2022/23 in order to cement his place in Wales' squad for the 2022 FIFA World Cup finals in Qatar.

BRENTFORD
KEANE LEWIS-POTTER

England U21 star Keane Lewis-Potter enjoyed an exceptional Championship campaign with Hull City in 2021/22 and that prompted Brentford to spend a club record fee to bring the exciting 21-year-old to West London.

A true attacker who can operate off of either flank, Lewis-Potter will be relishing the challenge of showcasing his skills at Premier League level.

BRIGHTON & HA
LEANDRO TROSSARD

After weighing in with eight Premier League goals last season, Belgian international winger Trossard has widely become recognised as the Seagulls' main creative force.

Hugging the left touchline and cutting inside to play in a teammate or striking for goal himself, Trossard is another player who will be looking to feature in the forthcoming World Cup.

CRYSTAL PALACE
WILFRIED ZAHA

Players may come and go at Selhurst Park, but the constant threat offered by the Crystal Palace club legend Wilfried Zaha remains firmly in place.

An exciting forward who loves to take opponents on in one-on-one situations, Zaha has now amassed over 400 appearances for the club across his two spells at Selhurst Park, and will be looking to fly the Eagles into the top half of the Premier League table.

CHELSEA
MASON MOUNT

Having progressed through the academy system at Stamford Bridge, attacking midfielder Mason Mount has become one of the first names on both the Chelsea and England teamsheet.

Mount hit eleven Premier League goals last season and head coach Graham Potter will be keen to see more of the same as Chelsea look to put pressure on Liverpool and Manchester City in 2022/23.

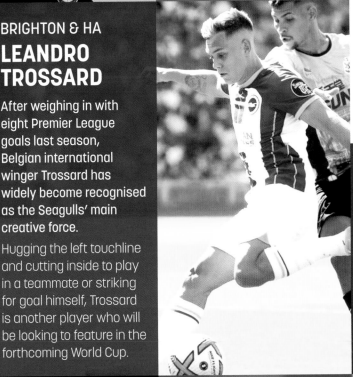

EVERTON
JORDAN PICKFORD

Firmly established as first choice keeper for club and country, Jordan has been a reliable last line of defence for the Toffees since joining the club in summer 2017.

A host of match-saving games last season were rewarded with the Player of the Season award and the England No.1 has now played over 200 games for Everton.

FULHAM
ALEKSANDAR MITROVIC

Having fired home a record-breaking 43 Championship goals for Fulham in their title-winning campaign last season, all eyes will be on Aleksandar Mitrovic in 2022/23.

If Fulham are to shake off their yo-yo club tag, then the top-flight goalscoring form of their powerful Serbian striker is going to be key.

LIVERPOOL
MOHAMED SALAH

Together with goalkeeper Alisson and inspirational defender Virgil van Dijk, Liverpool forward Mo Salah has been the catalyst for the Reds' success in recent seasons.

The Egyptian superstar jointly topped the Premier League scoring charts with Spurs' Son Heung-min last season as Liverpool enjoyed a domestic cup double.

LEEDS UNITED
PATRICK BAMFORD

After suffering an injury-hit 2021/22, Leeds United striker Patrick Bamford will be hopeful that 2022/23 offers him the chance to demonstrate the form that won him a first full England cap in September 2021.

A versatile front man who can play as a lone striker or in a pair, Bamford can also operate as an attacking midfielder from either flank.

LEICESTER CITY
JAMIE VARDY

The goalscoring hero of Leicester City's sensational 2014/15 Premier League title triumph, striker Jamie Vardy once again topped the Foxes' scoring charts last season.

An energetic forward, full of running, Jamie never gives defenders a moment of peace, and will once again be the one to watch for goals at King Power Stadium in 2022/23.

MANCHESTER CITY
ERLING HAALAND

Manchester City pulled off the biggest summer transfer coup when they lured Norwegian striker Erling Haaland from Borussia Dortmund to the Etihad Stadium for 2022/23.

Boasting a phenomenal strike rate at Dortmund and with his national team too, Haaland is sure to bring goals galore to the Premier League champions.

MANCHESTER UNITED
BRUNO FERNANDES

Attacking midfielder Bruno has become the heartbeat of the Red Devils' forward play since signing from Sporting Lisbon.

Blessed with a wide range of passing skills, the 28-year-old Portuguese international has the knack of unlocking even the tightest of defences.

TOTTENHAM HOTSPUR
SON HEUNG-MIN

South Korean superstar Son ended the 2021/22 season by picking up the Premier League Golden Boot as joint top goalscorer along with Liverpool's Mohamed Salah.

Forming an almost telepathic partnership with England captain Harry Kane, Tottenham Hotspur will certainly be a team to watch if Son repeats his lethal form in front of goal again in 2022/23.

NEWCASTLE UNITED
BRUNO GUIMARAES

After joining the Magpies from Lyon in January 2022, Brazilian midfielder Bruno has become a real cult hero with the fans at St James' Park.

Bruno scored five Premier League goals in 17 games last season and looks set to be one of the first names on Eddie Howe's teamsheet in 22/23.

NOTTINGHAM FOREST
DEAN HENDERSON

Forest made a real statement of intent following their promotion to the Premier League when they completed the season-long loan signing of the Man United keeper.

Capped by England, Dean will hope his City Ground performances can push him into England boss Gareth Southgate's thoughts for the 2022 FIFA World Cup finals in Qatar.

WEST HAM UNITED
JARROD BOWEN

Blessed with the ability to operate in a variety of attacking positions, Jarrod Bowen enjoyed an exceptional 2021/22 campaign.

The 25-year-old netted 18 goals in all competitions and made 51 appearances as the Hammers enjoyed a top-half finish and reached the semi-finals of the Europa League. He was also handed an England debut in June 2022.

SOUTHAMPTON
JAMES WARD-PROWSE

One of the very best dead ball deliverers, Saints skipper Ward-Prowse has progressed through the academy ranks at St Mary's to play over 350 first-team games for the club.

James is another England star who will hope to be on the plane for Qatar 2022.

WOLVES
GONCALO GUEDES

Wanderers boosted their attacking options when they completed the signing of Portugal forward Goncalo Guedes from Valencia at the start of the 2022/23 season.

Capped on over 30 occasions by Portugal, the 25-year-old is well known to Wolves' boss Bruno Lage having played for him at Benfica earlier in his career.

JOEL
VELTMAN
34

TRUE OR FALSE?

Here are ten fun footy True or False teasers for you to tackle!

Good luck...

ANSWERS ON PAGE 62

2. The FIFA World Cup in 2026 is due to be hosted in the USA, Mexico and Canada

3. Manchester City's former ground was called Maine Park

1. England star Harry Kane has only ever played club football for Spurs

4. Liverpool's Jurgen Klopp has never managed the German national team

5. Gareth Southgate succeeded Roy Hodgson as England manager

6. Manchester United's Old Trafford has the largest capacity in the Premier League

7. Jordan Pickford began his career at Everton

10. Leandro Trossard scored eight Premier League goals for Albion in 2021/22

8. Huddersfield Town's nickname is the Terriers

9. Albion defender Adam Webster was signed from Ipswich Town

NUMBER OF SEASONS
WITH THE SEAGULLS:

5

BRIGHTON & HOVE ALBION
LEAGUE APPEARANCES:

115

BRIGHTON & HOVE ALBION
LEAGUE GOALS:

10

PLAYER OF THE SEASON WINNER:

2009/10

LEGEND

ANDREW CROFTS

SEAGULLS ACHIEVEMENTS:

Was named captain in his first season
with the club and is now U21 coach

MAJOR STRENGTH:

Tough-tackling midfielder
with bags of energy

INTERNATIONAL ACTION:

Qualifying through one of his
grandparents, Crofts made 29 appearances
for Wales, having previously played
at U19 and U21 levels.

FINEST HOUR:

As a key member of the club's
coaching staff, he was made interim
first-team head coach following the
departure of Graham Potter

Andrew Crofts and Steve Sidwell
were real fans' favourites during their
playing days with the Albion, thanks to
their passion, commitment and high-level
performances from the heart of midfield.

Both hung up their boots to move into
coaching with the Seagulls, but who was
the better player?

It's another tight one to call...

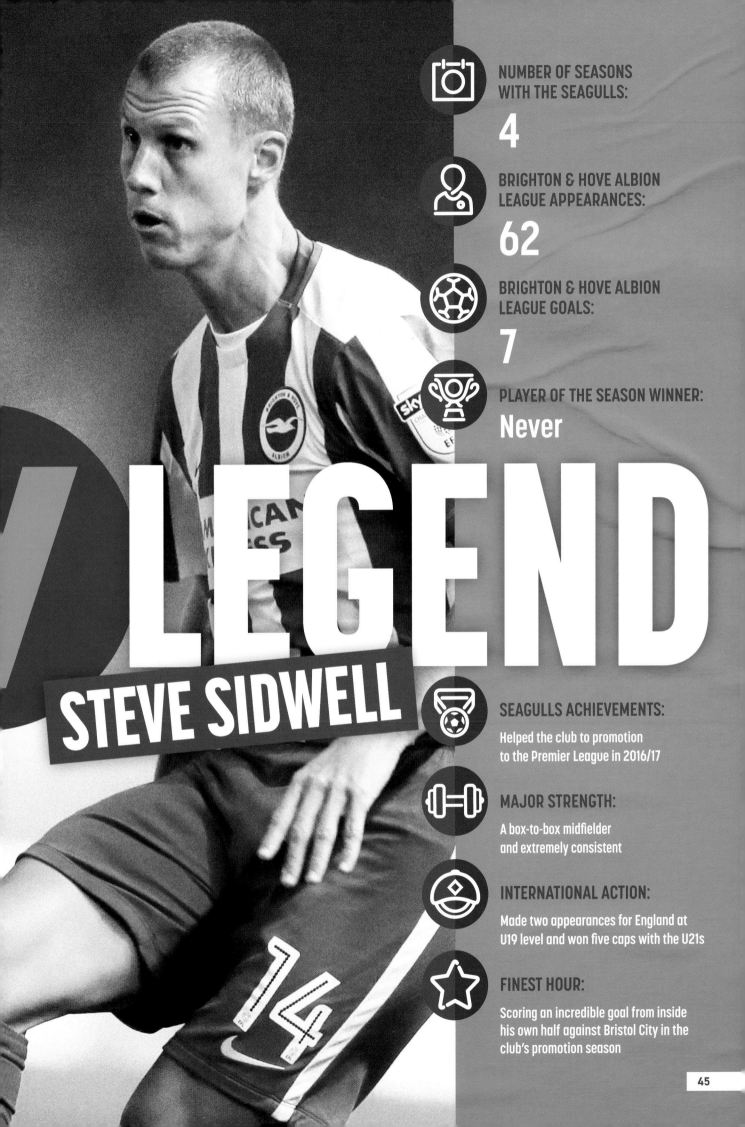

LEGEND
STEVE SIDWELL

NUMBER OF SEASONS WITH THE SEAGULLS:
4

BRIGHTON & HOVE ALBION LEAGUE APPEARANCES:
62

BRIGHTON & HOVE ALBION LEAGUE GOALS:
7

PLAYER OF THE SEASON WINNER:
Never

SEAGULLS ACHIEVEMENTS:
Helped the club to promotion to the Premier League in 2016/17

MAJOR STRENGTH:
A box-to-box midfielder and extremely consistent

INTERNATIONAL ACTION:
Made two appearances for England at U19 level and won five caps with the U21s

FINEST HOUR:
Scoring an incredible goal from inside his own half against Bristol City in the club's promotion season

CLUB SEARCH

EVERY TEAM IN THE PREMIER LEAGUE IS HIDDEN IN THE GRID, EXCEPT FOR ONE... CAN YOU WORK OUT WHICH ONE?

```
M  A  S  D  D  E  T  I  N  U  R  E  T  S  E  H  C  N  A  M
K  P  W  H  M  F  Y  A  G  I  S  G  F  Z  E  N  O  P  H  S
S  M  A  N  C  H  E  S  T  E  R  C  I  T  Y  J  B  F  O  E
W  N  A  E  L  T  G  I  R  C  I  A  S  B  D  R  I  U  J  T
K  E  F  R  U  P  S  T  O  H  M  A  H  N  E  T  T  O  T  G
H  Q  S  B  D  D  B  L  B  S  V  U  S  N  D  H  O  R  S  B
C  A  F  T  X  E  H  O  R  Y  S  N  T  H  A  K  J  M  E  E
A  G  Y  J  H  W  T  U  O  Q  C  F  N  M  C  A  L  V  R  C
U  O  U  T  S  A  R  I  L  P  O  D  P  K  L  P  E  A  O  A
H  T  S  U  I  G  M  A  N  R  A  T  P  L  U  R  T  D  F  L
T  P  T  H  P  C  N  U  D  U  O  M  I  S  T  A  F  E  M  A
U  I  T  W  V  E  R  A  N  N  E  V  F  O  W  E  P  G  A  P
O  R  M  E  S  J  W  E  P  I  N  L  N  L  E  S  U  L  H  L
M  O  K  R  O  S  U  V  T  O  T  A  T  M  N  L  C  I  G  A
E  M  A  H  L  U  F  G  T  S  K  E  K  S  D  E  B  M  N  T
N  N  L  D  Q  F  C  S  N  P  E  W  D  H  A  H  O  A  I  S
R  S  I  A  J  B  A  O  A  S  Y  C  B  O  O  C  N  X  T  Y
U  H  D  R  Z  L  O  O  P  R  E  V  I  L  U  L  W  J  T  R
O  T  E  C  D  E  T  I  N  U  S  D  E  E  L  R  A  E  O  C
B  R  I  G  H  T  O  N  &  H  O  V  E  A  L  B  I  O  N  T
```

Arsenal	Chelsea	Leicester City	Nottingham Forest
Aston Villa	Crystal Palace	Liverpool	Southampton
Bournemouth	Everton	Manchester City	Tottenham Hotspur
Brentford	Fulham	Manchester United	West Ham United
Brighton & Hove Albion	Leeds United	Newcastle United	Wolverhampton Wanderers

ANSWERS ON PAGE 62

11

LEANDRO
TROSSARD

WHICH BALL?

Can you work out which is the actual match ball in these two action pics?

ANSWERS ON PAGE 62

NAME THE SEASON

Can you recall the campaign when these magic moments occurred?

Good luck...

BRIGHTON & HOVE ALBION

ANSWERS ON PAGE 62

1. In which season did Chelsea last win the UEFA Champions League?

2. When were Manchester United last Premier League champions?

3. At the end of which season were England crowned World Cup winners?

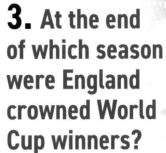

4. In which season did Aleksandar Mitrovic net 43 Championship goals for Fulham?

5. In which season did Leicester City become Premier League champions?

6. When did Tottenham Hotspur last reach the League Cup final?

7. In which season were Sheffield United last promoted to the Premier League?

8. When did Manchester City win their first Premier League title?

9. During which season did Lewis Dunk make his England debut?

10. In which Premier League campaign did Albion kick-off with a 3-0 opening day victory over Watford?

49

Albion
Women

After England's fantastic achievement in winning the women's UEFA European Championships in the summer of 2022, the profile of girls' and women's football continues to grow and grow.

With the Amex Stadium hosting three Euro 2022 matches, including two of the Lionesses games as they recorded a memorable 8-0 victory over Norway in the group stage and then edged past Spain in an epic quarter-final – Brighton certainly played its part in a great summer celebration of women's football.

At club level the Brighton & Hove Albion women's team continued to prosper in the Women's Super League in 2021/22 as they once again fought it out with England's top performing women's teams. Under the guidance of vastly experienced coach Hope Powell, the side recorded a seventh place league finish while also competing in the Women's FA Cup and League Cup competitions.

The 2021/22 campaign certainly started in impressive fashion for the Seagulls, who opened the season with a 2-0 win over West Ham United and then registered an emphatic 5-0 victory at Birmingham City to top the table after the second round of matches.

Other memorable results included a 2-1 victory at home to Tottenham Hotspur, a result which ended the London club's 100% winning start to the season and a goalless draw with defending league champions Chelsea.

Inessa Kaagman and Aileen Whelan ended the season as the team's leading scorers with four goals each, while the home match with Leicester City attracted the biggest home crowd of the season when 3,566 witnessed a 1-0 win over the Foxes at the Amex in November.

With the interest in the Seagulls' women's team continually on the up, the club continues to work in growing the women's game at all levels while providing a development pathway for young girls to benefit from.

Full details of the women's team and their 2022/23 fixtures can be found on the club's official website brightonandhovealbion.com

1. WHO AM I?

2. WHO AM I?

3. WHO AM I?

4. WHO AM I?

ANSWERS ON PAGE 62

WHO ARE YER?

Can you figure out who each of these Seagulls stars is?

5. WHO AM I?

6. WHO AM I?

7. WHO AM I?

8. WHO AM I?

5

LEWIS
DUNK

TRUE COLOURS

Can you colour
in this picture
of Lewis Dunk?

CHAMPIONSHIP WINNERS
Millwall

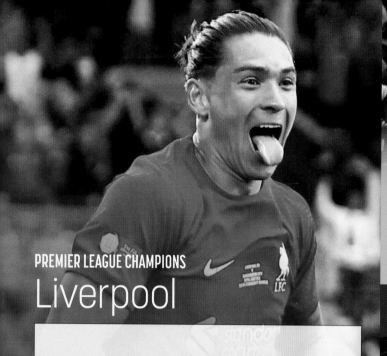

PREMIER LEAGUE CHAMPIONS
Liverpool

FAST FORWARD>>

Do your predictions for 2022/23 match our publisher's..?

CHAMPIONSHIP

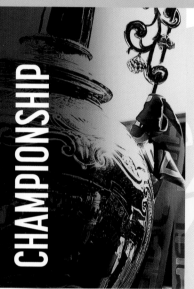

CHAMPIONSHIP RUNNERS-UP
Norwich City

PREMIER LEAGUE RUNNERS-UP
Chelsea

PREMIER LEAGUE

PREMIER LEAGUE TOP SCORER
Erling Haaland

CHAMPIONSHIP TOP SCORER
Michael Obafemi

LEAGUE ONE TOP SCORER
Conor Chaplin

FA CUP

FA CUP WINNERS
Brighton & HA

LEAGUE CUP WINNERS
Leicester City

LEAGUE CUP

LEAGUE ONE CHAMPIONS
Derby County

CHAMPIONS LEAGUE

CHAMPIONS LEAGUE WINNERS
Real Madrid

LEAGUE ONE RUNNERS-UP
Oxford United

LEAGUE ONE

EUROPA LEAGUE WINNERS
Roma

EUROPA LEAGUE

NUMBER OF SEASONS WITH THE SEAGULLS:

3

BRIGHTON & HOVE ALBION LEAGUE APPEARANCES:

139

PLAYER OF THE SEASON WINNER:

Never

SEAGULLS ACHIEVEMENTS:

EFL Championship
runners-up
2016/17

LEGEND

DAVID STOCKDALE

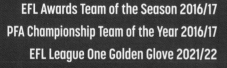

PERSONAL ACHIEVEMENTS:

EFL Awards Team of the Season 2016/17
PFA Championship Team of the Year 2016/17
EFL League One Golden Glove 2021/22

MAJOR STRENGTH:

Making himself big enough to cover
most of the width of the goal

INTERNATIONAL ACTION:

Apart from playing once for the
England 'C' team in 2004, Stockdale
never got a taste of international football

FINEST HOUR:

Being named in the Professional
Footballers' Association (PFA)
Championship Team of the Year
in 2017

In David Stockdale and Michel Kuipers,
we have two excellent goalkeepers. Not
only that, but they each became real
servants to the club during their respective
spells on the south coast.

Kuipers was with the club for an entire decade, and
while Stockdale's career took him all over the place,
most of his plaudits came during his Brighton days.

**But who had the edge as the best
Seagulls goalkeeper?**

LEGEND

MICHEL KUIPERS

NUMBER OF SEASONS WITH THE SEAGULLS:

10

BRIGHTON & HOVE ALBION LEAGUE APPEARANCES:

247

PLAYER OF THE SEASON WINNER:

Never

SEAGULLS ACHIEVEMENTS:

Football League Third Division winners 2000/01

Football League Second Division winners 2001/02

PLACE IN ALBION FOLKLORE:

Achieved in November 2002, he pulled off a save in a match at Wolves considered by many Albion fans to be the best-ever made by a Seagulls goalkeeper. His double-save saw him deny Alex Rae's powerful, goal-bound effort before getting up instantly to block Kenny Miller's follow-up - destined for the top, left-hand corner - with a powerful right arm.

MAJOR STRENGTH:

Quick reactions and reflexes to save from close range

INTERNATIONAL ACTION:

Kuipers never played for his native Netherlands with an elite band of Dutch goalkeepers around at the time

FINEST HOUR:

Saving a penalty against Manchester City in the League Cup in 2008

IDENTIEY THE STAR

Can you put a name to the football stars in these ten teasers?

Good luck...

ANSWERS ON PAGE 62

1. Manchester City's title-winning 'keeper Ederson shared the 2021/22 Golden Glove award for the number of clean sheets with which Premier League rival?

2. Which Portuguese superstar re-joined Manchester United in the 2021/22 season?

3. Can you name the Brazilian forward who joined Aston Villa in May 2022 following a loan spell at Villa Park?

4. Who became Arsenal manager in 2019?

5. Who scored the winning goal in the 2021/22 UEFA Champions League final?

6. After 550 games for West Ham United, which long-serving midfielder announced his retirement in 2022?

7. Who took the mantle of scoring Brentford's first Premier League goal?

8. Who scored the final goal for Manchester City in their 2021/22 Premier League title-winning season?

9. Can you recall Brighton's first Premier League goalscorer from the 2021/22 season?

10. Can you name the young Seagulls' defender who has been loaned to Derby County for the 2022/23 campaign?

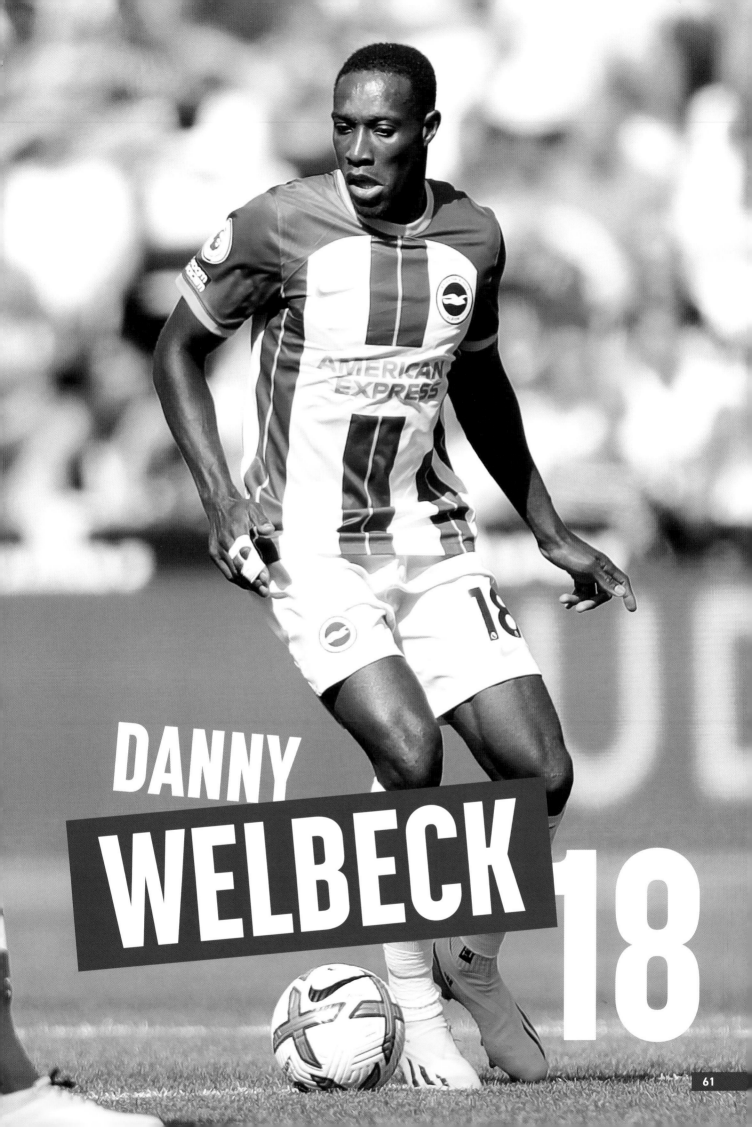

DANNY
WELBECK
18

ANSWERS

PAGE 26 · MULTIPLE CHOICE

1. C. 2. B. 3. A. 4. B. 5. C. 6. A. 7. B. 8. B. 9. A. 10. C.

PAGE 28 · FAN'TASTIC

PAGE 43 · TRUE OR FALSE?

1. False, Harry played on loan for Leyton Orient, Millwall, Norwich City & Leicester City. 2. True. 3. False, it was called Maine Road. 4. True. 5. False, Gareth succeeded Sam Allardyce. 6. True. 7. False, Jordan began his career at Sunderland. 8. True. 9. False, he was signed from Bristol City. 10. True.

PAGE 46 · CLUB SEARCH

Wolverhampton Wanderers

PAGE 48 · WHICH BALL?

PAGE 49 · NAME THE SEASON

1. 2020/21. 2. 2012/13. 3. 1965/66. 4. 2021/22. 5. 2015/16. 6. 2020/21. 7. 2018/19. 8. 2011/12. 9. 2018/19. 10. 2019/20.

PAGE 52 · WHO ARE YER?

1. Adam Webster. 2. Danny Welbeck. 3. Moises Caicedo. 4. Enock Mwepu. 5. Leandro Trossard. 6. Solly March. 7. Tariq Lamptey. 8. Alexis Mac Allister.

PAGE 60 · IDENTIFY THE STAR

1. Allison Becker. 2. Cristiano Ronaldo. 3. Philippe Coutinho. 4. Mikel Arteta. 5. Vinicius Junior. 6. Mark Noble. 7. Sergi Canos. 8. Ilkay Gundogan. 9. Neal Maupay. 10. Hayden Roberts.